International Food Library

FOOD IN
ISRAEL

International Food Library

FOOD IN
ISRAEL

text by
Nancy Loewen

recipes compiled by
Judith A. Ahlstrom

Rourke Publications, Inc.
Vero Beach, Florida 32964

© **1991 Rourke Publications, Inc.**

Library of Congress Cataloging-in-Publication Data

Loewen, Nancy, 1964-
   Food in Israel / by Nancy Loewen
     p. cm. — (International food library)
   Includes index.
   Summary: An introduction to Israel, its festivals, food customs, and cooking—derived from many cultures as Israel is a nation of immigrants.
   ISBN 0-86625-349-1
   1. Cookery, Israeli—Juvenile literature.   2. Cookery, Jewish—Juvenile literature.   3. Food habits—Israel—Juvenile literature. [1. Cookery, Israeli. 2. Cookery, Jewish. 3. Food habits—Israel. 4. Israel.]   I. Title.   II. Series.
TX724.L624   1991
641.595694—dc20   90-48797
                                                 CIP

PRINTED IN THE USA   AC

CONTENTS

AN INTRODUCTION TO ISRAEL

It is late afternoon in Jerusalem, Israel. Jewish worshipers pray before the 2,000-year-old Wailing Wall, the remains of an ancient Jewish temple. Arabs in white turbans barter for chickens and fruit at a crowded alley bazaar in Old Jerusalem. In the northern part of the city, construction workers busily shout orders as they build a new apartment building.

Like its best-known city, Israel is a mix of solemn ritual and unlimited energy. It is the biblical Holy Land, the setting for many of the events described in the Old and New Testaments. At the same time, Israel is a very young nation, having been created in 1948. It is a modern homeland for the Jews, but its cities and

The Wailing Wall in Jerusalem is a center for Jewish worshipers.

landmarks have religious meaning for Christians and Muslims as well.

Israel is located at the eastern end of the Mediterranean Sea. It is a tiny country, occupying an area of 8,020 square miles—slightly smaller than the state of Massachusetts. It is bordered by Egypt on the south and west and by Syria and Jordan on the east. Lebanon lies to the north.

Israel's climate and landscape vary from region to region. The area along the Mediterranean coast is very fertile, with hot summers and mild winters. This region is the center for Israel's agriculture and industry. It is the home of two of Israel's biggest cities, Haifa and Tel Aviv. Jerusalem, Israel's capital, lies nestled in the rolling Judean Hills in the central part of the nation.

The southern part of Israel consists of the triangle-shaped Negev Desert, Israel's driest region. The Rift Valley, located along the eastern border, is a rugged area formed when the earth's surface broke apart millions of years ago. Most of the valley lies below sea level.

AGRICULTURE & INDUSTRY IN ISRAEL

Israeli farmers produce more than three-fourths of their nation's food, which is quite an accomplishment. Israel has very little arable land—that is, land that can be used to grow crops. Over the past decades, however, the Israelis have increased their cropland by draining swamps, expanding irrigation, and practicing soil and water conservation techniques. In addition, scientists have taught farmers how to use each acre as efficiently as possible. Israel's main crops include oranges, cotton, tomatoes, melons, potatoes, and wheat. Cattle and poultry are the most common livestock raised.

Very few Israeli farmers own their land. Most belong to farming communities called *moshavim* or *kibbutzim*. In a moshav, families live and work separately but depend on their village administration to provide them with equipment and to sell their produce. In a kibbutz, all

Many of Israel's kibbutzim raise cattle.

Oranges are an important crop in Israel. In fact, when oranges are in season, Israeli hotels are required by law to serve fresh orange juice!

property and labor is shared equally. Members (*kibbutzniks*) have their own sleeping quarters, but share their meals in a community dining hall. In some kibbutzim, the children are raised in a separate home and see their parents for just a few hours each day.

Manufacturing employs more than four times as many people as agriculture. Important products include textiles, cut diamonds, metal and plastic products, and processed foods. Tourism, too, is a major industry in the Holy Land, generating $1.3 billion each year.

One of Israel's most unusual features is also an important natural resource. The Dead Sea—actually a salt lake—is located at the southern edge of the Rift Valley. At nearly 1,300 feet below sea level, it is the lowest point on the earth's surface. Potash, used to make fertilizer, is mined from the Dead Sea, along with other chemical salts. Copper and phosphates are mined nearby in the Negev Desert. Other mineral resources include clay, manganese, sulphur, gypsum, and a high grade of sand that is used to make glass.

ISRAELI FESTIVALS

Jewish holidays are an essential part of Israeli culture. Many are connected with historical events, and also with the passing of the seasons. *Rosh Hashanah*, the Jewish New Year, falls in September or October. It is marked by the blowing of the ram's horn, or *shofar*, in the synagogues. Ten days later comes *Yom Kippur*, the Day of Atonement. For Jews, this is the holiest day of the year. No food is eaten on Yom Kippur, and the entire country virtually shuts down.

Sukkot, or the Feast of the Tabernacles, is an eight-day harvest festival. During Sukkot, families eat their meals outdoors in small booths decorated with leaves, fruits, or vegetables. The booths represent the shelters the early Jews built while waiting to enter the Promised Land. *Hanukkah*, or the Festival of Lights, is celebrated around Christmastime. It dates back to the second century B.C., when the Jews defeated a Syrian ruler who had outlawed Jewish practices.

Jewish worshipers congregate at Jerusalem's Wailing Wall during *Sukkot*, the Feast of the Tabernacles.

Shavuot—a Jewish harvest festival—is sometimes observed with a special dance performance.

Pesach, or the Passover, marks the exodus of the Israelites from Egypt. It is the main springtime festival. *Shavuot*, or the Feast of Weeks, celebrates the first fruits of harvest. It also commemorates the revelation of the *Torah*, or sacred Jewish scriptures, to Moses on Mount Sinai.

The Muslims, too, have many religious holidays. The most important one is the month of *Ramadan*, which marks the time when the prophet Muhammad received the *Koran*, or the holy book of Islam. For the entire month, Muslims eat nothing between sunrise and sunset. At the end of Ramadan the people celebrate with a three-day feast.

Christmas and *Easter* are the main religious holidays for the Christians. On Christmas Eve, choirs from all over the world sing in Manger Square in Bethlehem. During the Holy Week of Easter, Jerusalem is filled with believers walking the Via Dolorosa, thought to be the path Christ took as he walked to the cross.

15

FOOD CUSTOMS IN ISRAEL

Israel is a nation of immigrants, and its cooking reflects many different cultures. One common factor, however, is the influence of Jewish dietary laws. These laws date back to the time of the Old Testament, and are still observed by many Jews. Food is said to be *kosher* when it is prepared or served according to these laws. Some foods, such as pork and shrimp, are strictly forbidden. Other foods can't be eaten in certain combinations. For instance, no dairy products (such as milk, butter, or cheese) may be served with any kind of meat. Orthodox Jewish households must even have two separate sets of serving dishes and utensils—one for meat dishes and one for milk dishes.

The observance of the Sabbath, too, has influenced Israeli cooking. The Jewish Sabbath begins at sundown on Friday night and ends at sundown on Saturday night. During this time, no work may be done. Some

The open market is a fact of life in Israel, attracting both tourists and natives.

16

Breakfast in Israel includes a wide variety of foods, as shown by this hotel's breakfast buffet.

Jewish families eat only cold foods, such as yogurt or salads. Many others eat a Sabbath casserole that is assembled on Friday afternoon and put in a low oven until the following day. This casserole, called *cholent* by the eastern European Jews, has many variations. It usually contains beef or mutton, potatoes or grains, and some type of beans.

Israeli cooking makes use of the fruits, vegetables, and dairy products that Israel has in abundance. Fresh salads or stuffed vegetables accompany most meals. Israelis usually don't eat very much red meat—chicken or fish are more common. More popular yet, especially during the hot summers, are light meals that make use of cheeses, vegetables, and breads.

The heartiest meal of the day is likely to be breakfast. This is a tradition that developed in Israel's kibbutzim, where members would get up very early, work several hours in the fields, and then sit down to an enormous feast.

17

Desert Shish Kebabs, ready to be broiled

Desert Shish Kebab

1 1/2 cups olive oil
1/3 cup wine vinegar
juice of 2 lemons
1 garlic clove, minced
1 onion, chopped
1 onion, cut in 1-inch square pieces
1 1/2 teaspoons salt
1 1/2 teaspoons oregano
1 teaspoon pepper
1/2 teaspoon ground thyme
2 pounds beef sirloin or lamb, cut in 1-inch cubes
1 green pepper, cut in 1-inch square pieces
12 whole mushrooms
12 cherry tomatoes

1. In a large glass cake pan or bowl, mix the oil, vinegar, lemon juice, garlic, chopped onion, and spices. Add meat and stir well. Cover and refrigerate 24 hours. Stir occasionally.
2. Alternate meat with vegetables on skewers.
3. Broil 4–5 minutes on each side. Serves 6.

Fried Rice

2 cups white long grain rice
2 tablespoons olive oil
1/2 teaspoon saffron
1 teaspoon salt
4 cups chicken broth
1/4 cup pine nuts
1/4 cup fresh parsley, chopped

1. Heat the oil in a large pan that has a tight-fitting cover. Add the rice and sauté for 2 minutes.
2. Turn heat to simmer. Add the saffron, salt, and chicken broth. Cover and cook 20–25 minutes or until all the liquid is absorbed. Just before serving, toss rice with pine nuts and parsley. Serves 6.

Cheesecake

2 cups crushed graham crackers, sprinkled with
    a little water to moisten
4 eggs, beaten
1 cup sugar
2 teaspoons vanilla extract
1 1/2 pounds cream cheese
1 cup sour cream

1. Line the bottom of a pie pan with crushed graham crackers.
2. Mix together the eggs, sugar, 1 teaspoon vanilla, and cream cheese. Pour over crust and bake 25 minutes at 375°.
3. Cool the cheesecake for 15 minutes. Turn the oven up to 475°.
4. Mix sour cream and 1 teaspoon vanilla, spread on top of cheesecake, and bake 5 minutes more. Chill overnight. Serves 6.

A SABBATH MEAL

Avocado and Fruit Salad
Cholent
Fresh Bread

By tradition, cholent is served on the Sabbath because it can be prepared in advance and cooked slowly in the oven. This version is much faster to make, but just as tasty.

Cholent

> 1 cup dried lima beans
> 3 pounds beef brisket
> 2 onions, chopped
> 1 tablespoon chicken fat
> 1 tablespoon salt
> 1/2 teaspoon pepper
> 1 teaspoon paprika
> 1 clove garlic, minced
> 5 cups hot water
> 1 cup kasha (buckwheat groats)

1. Soak beans in water for 12 hours.
2. In large pan, sauté the meat and onions in chicken fat until brown. Add salt, pepper, paprika, garlic, water, and drained beans. Cover and cook over low heat for 2 hours.
3. Add buckwheat. If needed, add a little more water. Cook 1 more hour or until brisket is tender.
4. Slice meat, and serve with beans and buckwheat. Serves 6–8.

**Avocado and Fruit
Salad**

Avocado and Fruit Salad

>   *1 grapefruit*
>   *2 small tangerines*
>   *3 pineapple rings*
>   *1 avocado*
>   *¹/₄ pound green grapes*
>   *vinaigrette salad dressing*
>   *curry powder*
>   *sugar to taste*

1. Peel the grapefruit and tangerines; divide into sections. Cut the pineapple rings in half. Peel the avocado and cut into strips.
2. Combine the grapefruit, tangerines, pineapple, and grapes in a bowl. Toss with vinaigrette dressing mixed with curry powder and sugar to taste.
3. Top with avocado slices and chill for at least 1 hour. Serves 6–8.

BLINTZES

Israelis from the United States and Europe brought the tradition of making blintzes with them. A blintz is a thin pancake filled with cheese, fruit, or meat. These recipes are for dessert blintzes. The recipe for making the pancakes is followed by recipes for three fillings.

Blintzes

3/4 cup flour
1/2 teaspoon salt
2 eggs, beaten
1 cup milk
1 tablespoon melted butter
fillings (see following recipes)

1. Mix the flour and the salt in a large bowl. Add eggs, milk, and butter. Beat until smooth.
2. Melt butter in a small (about 6-inch) frying pan on medium heat. Pour enough batter for a thin pancake; tilt the pan so the batter is spread evenly.
3. Cook until top looks dry. Remove from pan using spatula and place between layers of wax paper. This should be enough batter to make 12 blintzes.
4. Place filling in center of blintz. Fold blintz to enclose filling. Return to frying pan and cook on each side until brown. Serves 6.

Cheese Filling for Blintzes

2 cups cottage cheese
1 egg, beaten
1 teaspoon melted butter
1 teaspoon grated lemon rind
1 teaspoon vanilla
2 teaspoons sugar

1. Combine all ingredients and mix well. Use 2 tablespoons of filling per blintz. Top with whipped cream and fresh fruit.

Apple Filling for Blintzes

2 cups canned, sliced apples, drained
1 tablespoon ground almonds
1/4 teaspoon salt
1 tablespoon brown sugar
1/2 teaspoon cinnamon
1 tablespoon lemon juice
1 egg white, unbeaten

1. Combine all ingredients and mix well. Use 2 tablespoons of filling for each blintz. Top with sour cream and apple slices.

Cheese Blintzes

Blueberry Filling for Blintzes

1 1/2 cups canned blueberries, drained
1 1/2 tablespoons flour
1 tablespoon sugar
1/4 teaspoon cinnamon

1. Combine all ingredients and mix well. Use 2 tablespoons of filling for each blintz. Top with whipped cream and blueberries.

AN EVERYDAY MEAL

Falafel

If Israel has such a thing as a national dish, it is probably falafel.

1/3 cup chick-peas (also called garbanzo beans)
1/4 teaspoon baking soda
5 cloves garlic, chopped
1 teaspoon onion, chopped
1 teaspoon parsley, chopped
1/4 cup soybean flour
1/2 slice bread, torn up and sprinkled with water
2 teaspoons baking powder
1 teaspoon lemon juice
1 teaspoon salt
1 teaspoon paprika
1 teaspoon cumin
oil for deep frying
4–6 pitas (pocket breads), cut in half

1. Cover chick-peas with water and stir in baking soda. Soak overnight.
2. Drain the chick-peas. Add garlic, onion, and parsley. Put through a grinder or food processor.
3. Add the flour, bread, baking powder, lemon juice, salt, paprika, and cumin. Mix well.
4. Shape into 1-inch balls and deep fry in oil until golden brown.
5. Serve in pita, topped with chopped tomatoes, cucumbers, and tahina sauce. Serves 4–6.

GLOSSARY OF COOKING TERMS

For those readers who are less experienced in the kitchen, the following list explains the cooking terms used in this book.

Chopped	Cut into small pieces measuring about ½ inch thick. Finely chopped pieces should be about ⅛ inch thick.
Diced	Cut into small cubes.
Garnished	Decorated.
Grated	Cut into small pieces by using a grater.
Greased	Having been lightly coated with oil, butter, or margarine to prevent sticking.
Knead	To work dough with one's hands.
Marinate	To cover and soak with a mixture of juices, called a marinade.
Minced	Chopped into very tiny pieces.
Pinch	The amount you can pick up between your thumb and forefinger.
Reserve	To set aside an ingredient for future use.
Sauté	To cook food in oil, butter, or margarine at high temperature, while stirring constantly.
Shredded	Cut into lengths of 1–2 inches, about ¼ inch across. Finely shredded ingredients should be about ⅛ inch across.
Simmer	To cook on a stove at the lowest setting.
Sliced	Cut into thin slices that show the original shape of the object.
Toss	To mix the ingredients in a salad.
Whisk	To beat using a hand whisk or electric mixer.

ISRAELI COOKING

To make the recipes in this book, you will need the following equipment and ingredients, which may not be in your kitchen:

Cheeses Mozzarella, gouda, or cream cheese can be bought at a large supermarket.

Chicken broth Canned chicken broth is easy to find in the soup section at a supermarket.

Chicken fat About the only way to get this fat is by saving some when you cook chicken. You can substitute butter or margarine.

Chick-peas Also known as garbanzo beans, they can be found in most large supermarkets or health-food stores.

Kasha Also known as buckwheat groats, this grain can be found in many supermarkets and most health-food stores.

Matzo meal Can be found in supermarkets or Jewish food stores.

Pine nuts Will be found in the produce section of large supermarkets or in health-food stores.

Pitas Also called "pocket bread," it can be found in most supermarkets.

Soybean flour Most likely found in health-food stores.

Tahina Sometimes spelled tahini, this peanut-flavored sauce is found in health-food stores and large supermarkets.

Spices Cumin, curry powder, nutmeg, saffron, cinnamon, and vanilla extract will be found with other spices at a supermarket.

Customers line up to buy fresh strawberries at an outdoor market.

INDEX

We would like to thank and acknowledge the following people for the use of their photographs and transparencies:

Mark E. Ahlstrom: cover inset, 21, 22, 25, 27, 28; Israel Government Tourist Office: cover, 2, 7, 8, 9, 10, 11, 12, 13, 14, 15, 16, 17, 18, 19, 30.

Produced by Mark E. Ahlstrom (The Bookworks)
Typesetting and layout by The Final Word
Photo research by Judith Ahlstrom